FLIGHT FOR FREEDOM

Karny Wilson
Adventure Series
Book One

M G POLK

TEACHER GUIDE
Dr. Geraldine Polk

TEACHER GUIDE:
FLIGHT FOR FREEDOM:
KARNY WILSON ADVENTURE SERIES BOOK ONE
Copyright © 2021 Dr. Geraldine Polk and MG Polk

Flight for Freedom: Karny Wilson Adventure Series Book One
ISBN: 978-0-9890120-9-6 (Paperback)
ISBN: 978-0-9890120-8-9 (Ebook)

All rights reserved. No part of this book may be reproduced or used in any manner without written permission of the copyright owner except for the use of quotations in a book review, and for use as a teacher guide.

Cover Design, Typography & Production by Hallard Press LLC/John W Prince
Cover Images: Mark Ogee

Published by Hallard Press LLC.
www.HallardPress.com   Info@HallardPress.com
352-234-6099
Bulk copies of this book can be ordered at Info@Hallard-Press.com

ISBN: 978-1-951188-40-5

Printed in the United States of America

Publisher's Cataloging-in-Publication data

Names: Polk, Dr. Geraldine, author.
Title: Flight For Freedom: Teacher Guide / Dr. Geraldine Polk.
Description: The Villages, FL: Hallard Press, 2021. | Summary: Teacher Guide to accompany Flight For Freedom by Marcus G. Polk |Series: Karny Wilson Adventure Series. Book 1
Identifiers: ISBN: 978-1-951188-40-5 (print)
Subject: LCSH Polk, Marcus G. Flight For Freedom—Study Guides | Circus--Fiction. | Runaway children--Juvenile fiction. | Historical fiction. | BISAC JUVENILE FICTION / Action & Adventure / General | JUVENILE FICTION / Boys & Men | JUVENILE FICTION / Performing Arts / Circus | JUVENILE FICTION / Social Themes / Runaways | STUDY AIDS / Study Guides

Classification: LCC PZ7.1.P64282 Ad 2021 | DDC [Fic]--dc23

Flight for Freedom:
Karny Wilson Adventure Series Book One

M G Polk

Teacher Guide
Dr. Geraldine Polk

This Guide is designed for 5th through 8th grades in areas of reading, writing, speaking, listening, and language arts. The Teacher Guide includes a summary, characters, settings, themes, social issues and values, selected vocabulary, and writing or research topics.

Discussion and responses can be written or oral, and individualized to meet differing educational needs and situations.

As a 37-year classroom veteran, Dr. Geri Polk has shared the joys of reading and language with thousands of students. During those years of experience in journalism, public speaking, yearbook sponsorship, and writing student curriculum at multiple grade levels, she has developed a favorite saying to her that applies to students and to herself: "Learning is a lifetime achievement."

Figurative language is a special focus of this novel. Topics include similes, metaphors, idioms, hyperboles, personification, colloquialisms, slang, and jargon. Throughout the Guide, chapter and page numbers are used to help locate information in the book.

Examples:

Vocabulary:

(chapter, page,) word, definition

(2,9) **crucial**; *very important or significant*

Figurative Language:

(chapter, page,) words, meaning

(14,141) **raining cats and dogs**; *raining very hard*

Discussion:

Question, chapter, pages, quotes from text

  1. Why did Karny want to leave Maxwell?

(1,1) hated school locked out of house, grounded, on restriction

(1,3) father left them, his sister does well in school and he doesn't

(1,4) skipping school, retained in middle school, friends all moved on, fighting

(1,7) wants to be free, fight with the three boys on the field

Book Summary

Almost sixteen, Karny Wilson was leaving for good. Now the folks in Maxwell, Tennessee would have to sneer at someone else. He was heading for a new life away from the jeers, heartache, and frustration he had known. Hopping a train at Maxwell's Hobo Jungle, he heads out of Tennessee for places unknown. He knew the boxcar he was riding would take him away from all his problems, and with the slightest bit of luck, he just might find his father who had abandoned him when he was four.

From the start of his trek, Karny finds adventure and challenges he never expected. He meets two hobos who know his father and where to find him. Following their lead, he heads south to Tampa, Florida to find the man he hates but has to find. Along the way, Karny learns these two hobos were much more than drifters. They had very special powers. Through miracles or magic that could not be explained, Karny was convinced they were above mortal men. More than once, their unique abilities would keep Karny safe and alive.

Bobby Leonard, a runaway from Forrest Park, Georgia, joins Karny on his journey. Bobby jumps the train in Atlanta to flee a life filled with ill treatment, neglect, and violence. The two meet, become friends, and together make their way to Tampa, finding jobs at the Barker Brothers Carnival. Little did the two boys know their journey, jobs, and new found friendship would bring them close to death and closer together.

But most surprising, Karny discovers a girlfriend, an ability to be successful working in the carnival, and a newly found relationship with his father. The first part of Karny Wilson's flight for freedom was completed.

Characters

Karny Wilson—Almost sixteen year old Karny is a big, strong, redhead who has had enough of living with his mom in small town Maxwell, TN. He hates the town, school, and his life there. He jumps a train going anywhere hoping to find the father who abandoned him when he was four. Along the way Karny encounters a new friend, ruffians who try and take his life, and angels who protect him. When he finally meets his dad in Florida, Karny realizes the journey was a path to strengthen his moral values in his quest for closure.

Jessie and **Tommy**—Two angels disguised as hobos in their earthly state who meet Karny on the train and guide and protect him on his search for his father. During his journey through the Hobo Jungles, his harrowing train ride, and his adventures at the carnival, these two angels reinforce Karny's values and faith in God.

Bobby Leonard—Thirteen-year-old Bobby is a wiry, tough, street wise boy fleeing an abusive, alcoholic grandfather who wants the boy out of his life as soon as possible. When Bobby hops aboard at the Atlanta train yard, Karny invites him to team up on his journey. As Karny mentors the younger boy they develop a unique and lasting friendship, and both boys benefit from Tommy and Jessie's help.

Big Carny—Karny's father, Calvin Haskins Wilson, abandoned his wife, son, and older daughter following suspicion of robbery at the Old Grist Mill. On the run, Big Carny rejoins a carnival where he hides from the law and continues his drinking, stealing, and conning people. His baseball career fails because of his behavior and Carny wishes for more, but struggles to change. Meeting his son initiates his desire to change and become a better person.

Big Billy—Billy Barker, owner of Barker Brothers Family Carnival and Attractions and Naomi's father, manages the carnival with a fair firm hand and strong values, and very carefully guards his daughter Naomi. He hires Karny and Bobby setting the scene for Karny to meet his father.

Naomi—Big Billy's attractive daughter who works in the carnival ticket booth dressed as a gypsy. Since her mother's death three years ago from a high wire accident, she and Big Billy have become very close. Naomi becomes friends with the two boys and a love interest for Karny.

Marie Wilson—Marie, Karny's mother and Calvin Wilson's ex-wife, struggles with the challenge of raising her son and daughter, Marti, while working two jobs. She strives to give both her children strong values and guidance, but only Marti is doing well. Mrs. Wilson is distraught when Karny runs away, but tries to understand his decision.

Sheriff Bob—Bob Morse is the sheriff of Maxwell, TN who initiates the search when Big Carny leaves following the murder. Bob was Marie's first love and lifetime friend who supports her during this struggle.

Pastor Richardson—The pastor of Karny's church who helped him establish many of the values his mother had tried to teach him. He has a strong effect on Karny's values and behavior.

Marti Wilson—Karny's older sister who excelled in school and is now attending college. She acted as a second mother while Mrs. Wilson worked. She was the star pitcher on the championship Maxwell High School BOYS baseball team and taught Karny how to play.

Uncle Fred—Mrs. Wilson's older brother who took Karny camping and mentored him while he was growing up.

Mr. Silvestri—Cincinnati Reds baseball scout who recruits Karny.

Track Kings—Thugs who assault Karny and Bobby at the tracks and the carnival.

Settings

Maxwell, TN—A small rural town located in the Tennessee Mountains. The story occurs in the late 1950s when most families had two parents and mothers worked at home. In these small communities, values were important and everyone knew each other.

Hobo Jungles—Wooded areas near the train tracks where shiftless and sometimes mean characters jumped off trains from their free rides and waited to catch another train leaving. Since the early beginning of the railroad system, these small makeshift villages were and have always been part of the American landscape. During hard economic times, men looking for work would hop the trains for free rides. Between rides they would rest, eat, sleep, and often hide in these jungles.

Trains—These long strings of railroad cars were driven by coal burning engines. Train yards were hubs allowing trains to couple and uncouple cars and quickly move large quantities of cargo across the country.

Barker Brother's Carnival—The carnival, owned by Big Billy, was a mid-sized entertainment venue with rides and attractions that traveled from town to town providing enjoyment for local citizens. In addition to the midway with booths and games, the carnival contained a petting zoo, pony rides, and other attractions for the younger children.

Themes

Forgiveness—Letting go of grudges and bitterness can help one to achieve peace, hope, gratitude, and joy. There are several levels of forgiveness for different characters. Karny misses having a father. As he grows older, the abandonment causes him to feel even lonelier because he's unlike other kids. He struggles to understand and then forgive his father. Mrs. Wilson is also lonely without her husband and holds on to the resentment of having to work two jobs to support her family. Bobby cannot forgive those in his past who have hurt him, but his relationship with Karny helps him move toward this goal.

Friendship—The relationship of mutual affection between two or more people is evident in multiple situations. Although Karny's sister Marti functions as a second mother with care and nurturing while their mother works, she is also Karny's friend. She teaches him to play baseball, fishes with him, and supports him.

Sheriff Bob and Marie have been friends since childhood and eventually became childhood sweethearts. Despite their breakup when Marie met Big Carny, and Bob married Nancy, he remains a close and supportive friend.

Tommy and Jessie become Karny's friends when they save his life with miracles and help him on his journey. They maintain that friendship and assistance even when they physically leave him.

Karny and Bobby develop a mutual friendship as Karny mentors Bobby and they travel together. Although Bobby often shows rude, inappropriate behavior, Karny is supportive and encouraging.

Naomi and Karny become girlfriend/boyfriend as they spend much time together under Big Billy's watchful eye. They share a special bond knowing of Tommy and Jessie's assistance. Bobby joins this group as a friend of each and continues to mature. While neither Karny nor Big Carny is ready for a friendship, they are beginning to establish mutual respect and understanding.

Faith—Confidence or trust in a person, thing, deity, or in the doctrines or teachings of a religion. It is also a belief that is not based on proof. Several characters exhibit faith. Karny is strongly guided by his value-based upbringing, demonstrated by his prayers, efforts to help Bobby, and forgiving his father. He also has tremendous faith in Tommy and Jessie. Mrs. Wilson has faith in

Karny's ability to be "on his own" despite her initial doubts. Big Carny shows faith in his son when he recommends the baseball scout, Mr. Silvestri, observe Karny for potential play in the minor leagues.

Big Billy shows tremendous faith in his handling of his wife's death and his parenting with his daughter, Naomi. He strictly observes Sunday, and demonstrates his Christian values as he manages the carnival. Naomi also shows her faith in Karny and her father. Although Bobby has little faith in anything, he does begin to trust Karny's support and guidance.

Social Issues

Alcoholism—Both Karny's father and Bobby's grandfather struggle with alcoholism, but the contrast in how they deal with it is evident. Big Carny regularly attempts to quit and acknowledges his struggle. Bobby's grandfather simply continues to drink and pushes his grandson to leave, thus solving his problem of caring for Bobby.

Single parent families—All three of the teens deal with single parent family issues, including abandonment, poverty, death, and abuse. Karny's father abandoned him when he was four and he, his mother, and sister Marti, try to survive financially and emotionally. Marti makes progress, but Karny struggles in school and socially, while Mrs. Wilson must work two jobs to meet expenses. Bobby's father leaves and then dies, forcing Mrs. Leonard to raise him alone. When she becomes ill, they must move in with her parents and Mrs Leonard dies shortly thereafter. Bobby suffers abuse from his alcoholic grandfather who does not work and does not want Bobby in the house. Naomi was 12 when her mother was killed in a circus accident and her father, Big Billy, has worked religiously to give her a proper upbringing. She misses her mother greatly and struggles with growing up.

Homelessness—Tommy and Jessie, and several others in the story appear to be homeless. But their circumstances reveal they are really more than mere mortals presenting themselves in this setting. The other hobos in this story, as well as many others without resources, are homeless. Bobby is initially homeless since he leaves and plans never to return. Karny could be considered homeless during his travels.

Bullying—Individually and jointly, Karny and Bobby experience bullying. Alone, Karny encounters threats and bullying at school while Bobby struggles growing up in a tough suburb of Atlanta. When they unite as friends on their journey to Tampa, they both are accosted by the Track Kings who threaten to kill them. Later at the carnival, Karny is threatened by one of the thug's father and Bobby is threatened by the thug and his uncle.

Smoking—Miss Sally's smoking offends Big Billy who will not allow her to smoke when she is tutoring his daughter Naomi. Several of the other carnival workers smoke. While this was not a legal issue at the time is was still a point of conflict.

Values

Work Ethic—The majority of the characters believe in working for a living. Big Billy, Naomi, and the carnival workers all demonstrate this. So do Mrs. Wilson, Marti, Sheriff Bob, and Karny. Big Carny works when necessary but he is not above taking from others as is Bobby. Several of the hobos feel no shame in doing as little as possible to get by.

Stealing—Many of the ordinary hobos stole as did Big Carny, Bobby, and the Track Kings. When Karny criticizes Bobby about stealing, Bobby calls him a Holy Roller.

Fighting—The majority of the fighting involves self defense, especially for Karny.

At the ball field Karny bloodies the two boys who plan to gang up on him with their new pal. On the tracks in Tampa, Karny and Bobby defend themselves against the rock throwing Track Kings who want to kill them. Both Tommy and Jessie threaten the bullies in the hobo jungle to protect Karny. At the carnival they also assist Karny and Bobby when the boys are attacked. Big Carny engages in fighting at the Old Grist Mill when Danny threatens him. Bobby regularly engages in fighting in his neighborhood.

Lying—Karny's values deter him from lying, although he does avoid the truth when Detective Woods nearly arrests him to take him back to Maxwell. Bobby frequently lies but is trying to improve with Karny's help. Big Carny struggles with frequent lying, but is honest when he explains his past to his son.

Vocabulary

This section includes appropriate vocabulary for multiple grade levels, and development of more in depth analysis expected at higher levels. For vocabulary, use chapter and page numbers, the word and definition. Examples of vocabulary listing:

CODE	chapter #	pg#	word	definition
(2,9)	2	9	**crucial**	very important or significant
(6,41)	6	41	**unsavory**	distasteful, not pleasant
(21,205)	21	205	**alias**	assumed name

(1,2) **epiphany**—realization; a sudden intuitive leap of understanding, especially through an ordinary, but striking occurrence.

(1,2) **revelation**—disclosure; the revealing of something previously hidden or secret

(1,4) **scrutiny**—close, careful and

thorough examination or inspection

(1,7) **altercation**—heated argument, quarrel, or confrontation

(2,9) **crucial**—very important or significant

(2,13) **protruding**—to stick out from the surroundings

(2,13) **gingerly**—a very cautious, wary, or tentative way

(2,14) **scabbard**—a sheath, hanging from a belt, for a sword, dagger, or bayonet

(3,20) **apprehension**—arrest; takingc a criminal suspect into custody

(3,22) **anticipation**—the feeling of looking forward, usually excitedly or eagerly, to something that is going to happen

(4,25) **maneuvered**—to move or cause something to move skillfully

(4,25) **chain gang**—a group of prisoners who work away from the prison and are shackled together with leg irons and chains

(5,37) **disparaging**—showing or expressing disapproval or contempt

(6,40) **stature**—a person's standing height; somebody's standing or level of achievement

(6,40) **aggressively**—exhibiting determination, energy, and initiative

(6,40) **brandish**—to wave something about, especially a weapon, in a menacing, theatrical, or triumphant way

(6,41) **unsavory**—distasteful; not pleasant or agreeable

(6,41) **accosting**—to approach and stop somebody in order to speak to that person, especially in an aggressive or insistent way

(6,42) **deter**—restrain; to discourage somebody from taking action or prevent something from happening, especially by making somebody feel anxious

(7,47) **homicide**—the act or an instance of unlawfully killing another human being

(8,52) **dilemma**—a situation in which somebody must choose one of two or more unsatisfactory alternatives

(8,54) **inclement**—unpleasant in being stormy, rainy, or snowy

(9,57) **traversing**— to travel or move across, over, or through an area or place

(9,59) **reticent**—reserved; unwilling to communicate very much, talk freely, or reveal all the facts about something

(10,66) **carousing**—drinking and becoming noisy, especially in a group

(10,66) **navigating**—following a correct or satisfactory course along a route

(10,69) **raucous**—unpleasantly loud and harsh sounding

(10,70) **moochers**—individuals who steal or take from others

(10,76) **scot free**—without punishment exacted or payment being made

(10,76) **minors**—a league of teams that are not in the majors (especially baseball)

(10,77) **siesta**—an early afternoon nap or rest time

(11,84) **peripheral**—at or relating to the edge of something

(11,86) **insinuated**—to hint at something unpleasant or suggest it indirectly

(11,89) **humiliating**—damaging to somebody's dignity or pride, especially publicly

(11,90) **denizens**—a habitual visitor to a place

(11,90) **incoherent**—unable to express thoughts or feelings clearly or logically

(11,92) **salvation**—being saved or protected from harm

(12,97) **ingeniously**—in a clever, original, and effective way

(12,97) **semblance**—an outward appearance or imitation of something

(12,102) **sarcastically**—using words that mean the opposite of what they seem to mean and are intended to mock or deride

(12,104) **dumbfounded**—temporarily speechless with astonishment

(12,105) **perplexed**—puzzled or confused

(13,108) **muster**—to summon up something such as strength or courage that will help in doing something

(13,109) **slight-of-hand**—techniques to manipulate cards or coins secretly (the formal name is prestidigitation)

(13,112) **depicting**—showing something in a picture, painting, or sculpture

(13,114) **ransacked**—searched very thoroughly, but handled things carelessly

(13,115) **jaywalking**—crossing a street anywhere other than the designated crossing place. It is illegal in some places, though rarely prosecuted

(14,120) **cocoon**—something that covers or envelopes somebody or something in order to provide warmth or protection

(14,123) **silhouette**—something lit as to appear dark, but surrounded by light

(15,140) **ruffians**—rough, bullying, or violent individuals, often members of a gang

(15,141) **exasperated**—very angry or frustrated

(15,142) **lumbered**—moved clumsily or heavily

(16,149) **surefooted**—skilled and confident in moving or climbing, and so unlikely to stumble or fall

(16,150) **grimacing**—contorting or twisting the face to express disgust or pain

(16,164) **trepidation**—fear or uneasiness about the future or future events

(18,178) **stammering**—speaking with many quick hesitations or repetitions

(18,180) **assailant**—somebody who violently attacks someone else, causing injury

(18,180) **adversaries**—opponents in a conflict, contest, or debate.

(19,191) **onslaught**—a large quantity of people or things difficult to deal with

(20,193) **convoluted**—too complex or intricate to understand easily

(20,194) **oblivious**—unaware of or not paying attention to somebody or something

(20,199) **roustabouts**—unskilled laborers, especially on an oil-drilling rig, on a ship or wharf, or in a circus or carnival

(21,205) **alias**—an assumed name that somebody uses

(22,211) **fiasco**—a total failure, especially

humiliating or ludicrous

(22,214) **farm system**—a team or club whose role is to provide experience and training for young players, with an agreement that any successful players can move on to a higher level at a given point. This system can be implemented in many ways both formally and informally.

(22,218) **lucrative**—producing profit or wealth

QUESTIONS FOR DISCUSSION

This section includes questions that are appropriate for multiple grade levels through expansion of comprehension skills, development of more in depth analysis and responses at higher levels. Use chapter and page numbers as in the vocabulary to locate information and quote examples accurately from the text.

Example: (chapter and page numbers and suggested answers)

1 What did Mrs. Wilson do to make Karny go to school?
(1,2) Make Karny leave with her
(1,3) locked him out of the house
(1,3) gave Granny Baker the key
(1,4-5) referred to counselor for Crossroads

1.) Explain why Karny wants to leave Maxwell.
(1,1) hated school, locked out of his house, grounded, on restriction
(1,3) father left them, his sister does well in school and he doesn't
(1,4) skipping school, retained in middle school, friends moved on, fighting
(1,5-7) wants to be free, fight with the three boys on the field

2.) Describe how Karny sequences his escape plan. Analyze the effectiveness of the steps in his plan.
(2,9-11) plan ahead—lie about his age, get a job in the carnival, get transportation, mental list of what to take with him
(2,12-15) quietly approach, break the basement window, sneak upstairs, pack his duffle bag and sleeping bag, Swiss Army knife, and $76
(3,17-22) pack food, leave a note for his mom, sneak back out the window, head for the Hobo Jungle

3.) Compare and contrast how Marie Wilson reacts to Karny's leaving through her responses to Granny Baker, Karny, Sheriff Bob, and Martha.
(5,27-36) Granny—confused and upset when Granny tells her Karny has run away, guilty that she did not do enough for him, annoyed by Granny's comments
(5,29-31) Karny—understands his struggles, loves and misses him, angry he ran away, ashamed for her anger, worried about him
(5,32-37) appreciative of Bob's gentleman

behavior, help, and willingness to listen and support her

(7,48-49) Bob helps search for Karny, comforts Marie, who is embarrassed about her relationship with Big Carny

(6,32-34) Martha—eager to talk with her, frustrated when Martha asked if she knew about Karny's problems, apologetic for snapping at her

4.) Compare and contrast Karny's response to his meetings with Tommy and Jessie at the cane breaks and then in the boxcar. Describe how these interactions help explain the themes of faith and friendship.

(6,39-41) Cane break—Karny felt threatened when he met them and pulled his knife, he wanted no advice or help from them, very independent, scared

(10,66-79) Box car—Karny is surprised they saved him, nervous without his weapon, willing to accept help advice, eager to learn about his dad, glad for their support and friendship

5.) Explain how Marie Wilson describes Big Carny's actions the night of the murder. Quote evidence from the text.

(9,58-60) She knew Carny was planning to steal the money, he broke into the office to wait for Danny, When Danny came in with a gun and threatened Carny by name, he shoved Danny down and ran home. He told Marie Danny would be chasing him and wanted to kill him. He gave her some money and fled the county. Carny didn't know Danny was dead before he left Maxwell

6.) Explain how Karny's encounters with the police in Chattanooga at the fence and later in the box car affect his future.

(11, 84-86) Karny escaped from the cop at the fence, but had a physical confrontation and tore his backpack, cop threatened to arrest him, Karny escaped by pulling his backpack through the fence and running away

(13,113-118) Karny escaped from this cop, but with no physical contact, the cop knew Sheriff Bob and planned to escort Karny back home, detective was not threatening and did not use cuffs on Karny, He escaped when the cop was called to help his partner with the real thugs

7.) Evaluate the significance of Tommy and Jessie's help for Karny. How does this assistance help establish the themes of forgiveness, faith, and friendship?

(10,65-67) They pull Karny into the boxcar to save his life

(10,71-79) They inform Karny about his father, what he did, and how to find him

(10,78-79) They warn him of the dangers in Tampa

(11,92-95) They save him from the thugs as he enters the Chattanooga Jungle

(13,108-09) They provided new supplies to fill his duffle bag

(20,195-200) They save Karny and Bobby

from the assault by the uncle and father at the carnival.

8.) Examine the impact of baseball in Karny's life. How do his experiences with baseball determine his actions and reactions?

(2,14) Takes ball and glove when he runs away

(13,109-111) Marti was star player who taught Karny

(16,150-155) Karny and Bobby fight the Track Kings by throwing rocks

(22,211) Karny plays baseball with carnival league

(22,213-218) Scout comes to check out Karny and dad supports him

9.) Compare and contrast the four major settings in the story: Maxwell, hobo jungles, the trains, and the Barker Brothers' Carnival. How do these settings impact Karny's actions and responses to different situations?

Maxwell, TN—a small rural town located in the Tennessee Mountains. The story occurs in the late 1950s when most families had two parents and mothers worked at home. There was only one junior and one senior high school and most everyone knew each other. People watched out for one another as in many small towns.

Hobo Jungles—Wooded areas near the train tracks where shiftless and sometimes mean characters jumped off trains from their free ride and waited to catch another train leaving. Since the early beginning of the railroad system these small makeshift villages were and have always been part of the American landscape. During hard economic times men would hop the trains for free rides to places looking for work. Between rides men would rest, eat, sleep and often hide in these jungles.

Trains—These long strings of rail road cars driven by coal burning engines provided much of the nation's basic transportation and freight shipments. Huge rail yards were hubs allowing trains to couple and uncouple cars and quickly move large quantities of cargo across the country. Many strangers and hobos rode these trains and situations were often dangerous.

Barker Brother's Carnival—This carnival owned by Big Billy was a mid-sized entertainment venue with rides and attractions that traveled from town to town providing enjoyment for local citizens. In addition to the midway with booths and games, the carnival contained a petting zoo, pony rides and other attractions for the younger children. In the early days circuses and carnivals were not separate. These businesses included a wide variety of individuals with different backgrounds, customs, and skill. The camaraderie and sense of community was very strong.

10.) Compare and contrast the effects of living in a single parent family for Karny,

Bobby, and Naomi. How does this help clarify the themes of faith, friendship, and forgiveness?

Karny

(1,3) Karny's dad left the family and disappeared

(1,4) Karny's mom has full responsibility for work and family

(5,30-31) Mom works 2 jobs, spends less time with Karny

(7,48) Karny learned outdoor skills from Sheriff Bob and his uncle, not dad

(9,57-61) Big Carny was a drunk and a thief, bad role model

(10,79) Karny would search for his dad but wanted no relationship

(15,144) Karny's mom had to instill all moral values

(15,144-146) Karny needs to find and confront his father so he runs away

(18,173-174) Very stressful meeting his dad at the carnival

(21,205-208) Confused when finally talking with his dad, not sure what to do.

(22,218) finally forgiving his father and wants to try to build a new relationship

Bobby

(14,125) Bobby's grandfather beats and abuses him, does not support family

(14,125,126) Bobby's dad leaves, then dies; mom also dies

(14,126) Bobby plans to steal—poor moral values

(14,126) Bobby didn't care about anyone at home and no one cared for him

(16,151-154) Bobby is eager to fight and taunts others

(16,160-161) Bobby can hardly read or write; no formal education or support

(18,180,197) Bobby taunts the Track King bullies

(19,170,188,197) Bobby is streetwise, tough, and has to stand up for himself

(22,218) Bobby needs Karny's dad to sign paperwork, no family

Naomi

(17,179,193) Big Billy is a very strong in charge father, very little freedom for her, strong support for education and good behavior

(18,200) Billy warns Karny about his behavior around Naomi

(21,210) Naomi's mother died in a fall from the trapeze, no female figure

(22,212) Karny says Naomi's dad is "like a sheriff" because Big Billy has such very high standards for her

11.) Analyze how the author develops and contrasts the points of view for Karny and Naomi's relationship with each other.

Karny

(18,178-179) Does not want to talk to a girl, uncomfortable

(18,178) Thinks she is the prettiest female he has ever seen

(18,178,203) Awkward when speaking to Naomi

(18,185) Surprised about Big Billy's warning about Naomi

(19,187) Confused when he finds himself thinking about her often

(19,189) She reminds him of his sister – pretty, sweet, nice, best friend

(20,204) She smelled nice and was kind to him

(22,212) Steals a kiss

(22,212) Surprised she thinks of marriage before kissing

(22,213) Thinks Big Billy is a sheriff who watches too closely

(22,213) He will keep asking for kisses

Naomi

(18,179) She thinks Karny is cute, and notices how awkward he is when speaking to her; glad to see two boys her age working at the carnival

(18,179) She has been asked for dates by others but not interested

(19,211-12) She is helpful and supportive to Karny and Bobby

(20,200) She sees the ax handle change and agrees to keep the secret

(22,212) They are always together—school, baseball games, work and they hold hands when Billy is not looking

(22,212) She tells Karny stealing a kiss is dishonest

(22,213) She is glad her father is stern and looks out for her

(22,214-216) She asks Mr. Silvestri about his interest in Karny and is concerned about breaking his spirit

12.) Predict Karny's future in baseball.

13.) Explain how a particular series of events fit together and contribute to the theme of friendship by explaining how Karny mentors Bobby. (chapters 4-19)

14.) Explain the changes in Karny's relationships with his mother and his father

15.) Explain the actions and situations that lead Karny to question his belief that Tommy and Jessie are more than mere mortals.

16.) Explain how Karny's values and upbringing affect his interactions with other characters in the story. Include his parents, Bobby, Naomi, Tommy, and Jessie.

17.) Research hobos and hobo jungles. Research carnivals and/or circuses.

WORKING WITH FIGURATIVE LANGUAGE

These examples coordinate with *Flight for Freedom*, Karny Wilson Adventure Series, Book One. They can be found using chapter and page numbers as was done with vocabulary. Highlighting each type of figurative language in the book using a different color is very helpful for locating, identifying or grouping items. Pastel markers are best.

Simile	green	*Idiom*	yellow
Metaphor	blue	*Colloquialism*	yellow with green dot
Hyperbole	orange	*Slang*	yellow with pink dot
Personification	pink	*Jargon*	purple

Figurative Language

This novel focuses on figurative language. These literary devices are used to create a special effect or feeling by making an interesting or creative comparison using language as the key element.

Similes—comparison of two unlike thing using "like" or "as"
(11,91) as easy as pie—very simple

Metaphors—comparison of two unlike things with no comparing word
(2,11) car was a lemon—car was old and in very bad shape

Personification—giving human characteristics to inanimate objects, animals, or ideas
(2,14) quiet told him he was alone—lack of noise let him know he was by himself

Hyperbole—overstatement or exaggeration
(9,60) scared to death—extremely frightened

Idioms—well-known expressions that contain a figurative meaning that is different from the literal meaning of the phrase.
(18,182) **on the ball**—paying attention, doing things well

Colloquialisms, Slang, and Jargon are all forms of idioms.

(2,10) **It hit him**—he understood. Colloquialisms are more common in informal speech

(10,74) **High tail it**—run as fast as possible, especially when fleeing. Slang includes chiefly playful speech deliberatively used in place of standard terms

(2,10) **ox is in the ditch**—there is a problem with unavoidable work ahead. Jargon is a special vocabulary used by a group such as legal, religious, political, etc.

Similes

(1,2) **hard as pulling hen's teeth**—very difficult since hen's have no teeth
(2,9) **he felt like a prisoner**—they felt guilty and trapped
(2,13) **Karny was feeling like a criminal**—he felt guilty about his actions
(3,20) **stand out like a sore thumb**—be very obvious; everyone notices the difference
(6,39) **pants were as dirty as the white man's beard**—pants were filthy
(6,43) **as quick as a flash**—very fast
(8,54) **ridge worked like the gutters on a house**—edge was like rain gutters on a house
(10,66) **lights from vehicles were like beacons**—car headlights shone very brightly to guide him
(10,69) **laugh like a braying donkey**—a very loud, irritating laugh
(10,76) **sheriff came with bloodhounds like it was a double murder**—the sheriff came with the dogs as if this were a very serious case
(11,82) **tearing up like a baby**—showing emotion like a little child
(11,85) **as quick as a rabbit escaping a farmer's garden**—very fast
(11,87 **body looked like it was dipped in strawberry ice cream**—his body was all pink
(11,88 **he felt like a hunted animal**—he was scared
(11,88) **as easy as pie**—very simple
(11,89) **woods looked like a real jungle**—woods were very thick and dark
(11,90) **dirty as a used penny**—very dirty
(11,93) **as quick as a cat**—very fast
(11,94) **wood like a medieval weapon**—wood similar to an old fashioned weapon
(12,103) **big grins like kids in a candy shop**—their big smiles showed they were looking forward to enjoying the food being offered
(13,111) **dream was like a nightmare**—dream was very scary and not pleasant

(13,115) **one was as big and strong as a bear**—person was very large and powerful
(15,141) **hit the sand pile…it was like jumping into a soft bed**—it was a soft landing
(15,141) **jump like a rabbit**—jump quickly and steadily
(15,142) **run like a scared chicken**—run away like a frightened animal
(16,151) **pick them off like flies**—hit them one at a time like killing flies
(16,153) **as fast as lightning**—very quickly
(16,153) **he went down …like a dropped bag of potatoes**—he collapsed in a pile
(16,160) **black rimmed glasses that looked like they belonged on an old man**—glasses with dark frames that were more suitable for an older man
17,168) **as wide as a door**—very broad and large, especially in the shoulders
(18,178) **dress like a grownup**—dress in a way so one looks older than one really is
(18,182) **storming the place like Sherman took Atlanta**—rushing in like the Civil War General Sherman did when attacking the city of Atlanta
(20,196) **like a dog chasing rabbits**—move very quickly
(20,198) **spitting flames like a holiday sparkler**—flames came out like a sparkler
(20,198) **sounded like a two ton Clydesdale**—very loud noise as if from a huge horse
(20,199) **ran like a scalded dog**—ran very quickly
(22,212) **he's like a sheriff**—he always watches the moves people make
(22,213) **he's like the pa I never had**—similar to the father one never had
(22,216) **humans are like puzzles**—humans are very complicated
(22,217) **like a knot on a log**—completely inert
(22,218) **he's like an orphan**—he is all alone with no family

Metaphors

(1,1) **playing hooky was one of his favorite sports**—he really enjoyed skipping school
(1,3) **are you a warden**—his mom in charge of his prison
(2,11) **car was a lemon**—car was old and in very bad shape
(4,24) **He was… a crippled, darkened spirit**—he felt weak and badly about himself
(4,26) **slow moving iron horse was… his golden chariot to freedom**—the train was his way of leaving his problems and moving to new opportunities
(5,37) **mistakes were life's strongest lessons**—mistakes are powerful ways to learn
(7,48) **underwater walkway is an easy way out**—path under the water is the best way to get out with the least resistance
(10,67) **knife …this here toothpick**—knife was sharp and small like a toothpick

Teacher Guide: Flight for Freedom / Karny Wilson Adventure Series Book One by M G Polk

---

(10,68) **you were Gene Autry or Roy Rogers**—you behaved in a heroic manner like these popular cowboys did
(10,77) **he's bullet fast**—he is extremely fast
(11,87) **silence of the woods was music to his ear**— the quiet woods let him know he was safe
(11,88) **flow was…the hot tempered curse word**—breeze was bringing the sounds of the bad language into the room
(11,89) **pine trees formed a canopy**—trees were close together and covered the area
(11,93) **bigger one…seemed to be a 300 pound stinking bear**—taller man was big and smelly
(12,97) **Maxwell Hobo Jungle was not a tourist picture**—the jungle was dirty, messy
(13,109 **friends were some type of heavenly creatures**—the friends were superhuman; divine
(13,109) **creating something out of nothing was …a miracle**—making something without any materials was a marvel or even considered as a work of God
(13,111) **completing homework was impossible task**—finishing homework was very difficult
(13,114) **recent attack…was nothing compared to this emotional blow**—earlier attack was very small compared to this new situation
(14,132) **they (Tommy and Jessie) are ghosts**—the two men are not alive
(16,154) **lay that scoundrel out cold was a perfect strike**—knocking out the bully was great
(16,162) **carpet was natural grass**—there was no carpet, only grass
(18,179) **getting his approval was a monumental task**—getting agreement was difficult
(19,189) **my sister was my best friend**—his sister was very close to him
(21,202) **cooled evening air…was a relief for the hardworking crew**—cool air was pleasant for people who worked a long day in the heat
(21,202) **different characters sitting at the table or standing in line… was a sight to behold**—the different, unique people were very interesting to see
(22,211) **playing baseball until the Sunday service was over was blasphemy**—playing ball during the church service was sinful or extremely bad
(22,212) **stealing a kiss is dishonest**—taking a kiss without asking is not honest
(22,215) **professional baseball is a business**—pro baseball is more than a game, it's a job
(22,216) **man's character, his life, and his spiritual makeup is the puzzle which is his potential completeness**—a person's character, life, and relationship with their creator is the potential total that makes an individual complete

Teacher Guide: Flight for Freedom / Karny Wilson Adventure Series Book One by M G Polk

Personification

(1,5) **voice stirring him from his daydream**—sounds causing him to stop and listen
(2,13) **breaking glass sent an announcement**—sound let everyone know he was breaking in
(2,13) **quiet told him he was alone**—lack of noise let him know he was by himself
(4,24) **corn leaves spanking his clothes**—as he runs, the leaves hit him
(4,25) **machine alerted all the ten o'clock was on its way**—the train signal let everyone know the train was leaving the station at 10:00
(6,42) **squeal of steam... blast of whistle brought Karny's attention back**—the train noises stopped Karny's thoughts and helped him focus on where he was
(8,52) **shoes felt for the bottom of the ladder**—his feet tried to reach the bottom of the ladder
(8,53) **wind ...playing king of the hill**—the wind was pushing him to cause him to fall
(8,55) **train began to show its muscle**—the train started to speed up
(10,66) **darkness covered the mountain**—night caused the mountain to become dark
(10,66) **overcast clouds blanketed the moon and stars**—clouds covered the light from the moon and stars
(10,78) **thoughts were running through Karny's mind**—Karny had many ideas
(11,86) **sounds of cars telling him he was heading in the right direction**—the sound of the cars let him know he was moving in the correct direction
(11,87) **briars grab the legs of is jeans**—briars stick to his jeans
(11,90) **curiosity kept pulling them back**—wanting to know more brought them back again
(12,98) **stomach growled**—stomach made noises indicating hunger
(12,104) **flames... danced**—fire appeared to move like a dancer
(14,120) **train finished its lengthy boxcar dance**—train completed connecting all the boxcars
(14,121) **massive giant had begun its journey**—train started to move forward
(14,122) **dream was shattered**—dream stopped suddenly
(14,123) **time didn't tell him where he was**—watch could not indicate his location
(14,123) **thoughts were startled back to reality**—mind returned quickly to the present
(14,127) **night air swirled**—air moved about
(14,128) **mammoth puzzle continued steaming south**—the huge train continued traveling south
(14,128) **hours crept by**—time moved very slowly
(16,148) **plant burrs were attaching themselves to their pants legs**—burrs were sticking to their pants

(16,158) **cloud of smoke flowed out of the trailer**—smoke moved out from the trailer
(17,173) **animal telling you it wants to be brushed**—animal pushed his nose at the boy
(17,173) **wonder and hope, ridicule and shame came boiling up**—feelings reached a critical point and overwhelmed a person
(18,179) **gypsy attire gave the impression she was older**— costume made her look older and more mature
(20,194) **tickets were flying out of the booth**—tickets were moving quickly from seller to buyer
(20,195) **shrills from the kids… bring him back to his task**—noises from the children alert him about the job he is doing
(20,196) **animals were causing a small riot**—animals were creating a commotion

Hyperboles

(5,33) **worried sick**—very worried or concerned
(9,59) **relived that night a thousand times**—thought about that night many times
(9,60) **scared to death**—extremely frightened
(10,73) **Pa is known by everyone who jumped a train**—he is known by many people who rode the trains
(10,73) **name is on a thousand boxcars**—name is written on many boxcars
(11,93) **knocking it (your head) halfway to downtown Chattanooga**—strike his head extremely hard and send it moving in one direction
(12,103) **devoured in three bites**—ate very quickly
(13,107) **ton of questions**—many questions
(13,111) **millions of cracks**—many, many cracks
(13,116) **breakneck speed**—dangerously fast
(14,132) **everybody knew them**—many people knew them
(15,145) **nobody could ask for a better mother**—she is a great mother to Karny
(16,149) **spot 'em a mile off**—see a long distance
(16,151) **everybody in Georgia would pick on you**—many people in Georgia would bother you
(18,182) **a ton of little kids**—many young children
(20,193) **a million kids running crazy**—many children running around

(20,198) **in the blink of an eye**—extremely quickly

(21,202) **so hungry I could eat ponies**—very hungry

(22,216) **a ton of talent**—a great deal of talent

(22,216) **hundreds players never make the minors**—many do not make the minors

Idioms

(1,1) **add insult to injury**—to make a bad situation even worse

(1,1) **bitter pill (experience)**—disappointment; something hard to accept

(1,2) **a fly in the ointment**—something small that spoils one's fun

(1,2) **make something of**—improve; make something important

(1,3) **look up to**—honor or respect someone as a good example

(1,4) **to no avail**—unsuccessful; have no effect

(1,5) **ball is in your court**—up to you to make the next move

(1,6) **know better**—be smart enough not to do something

(1,6) **let off easy**—release someone with very little punishment

(1,6) **stop in one's tracks**—stop quickly or with great force

(1,7) **enough is enough**—that's the limit; no more

(2,9) **settle (down)**—begin to live a quiet and stable life

(2,10) **pass for**—be taken for; be considered as

(2,11) **get through**—finish

(2,11) **go to one's head**—be conceited

(2,12) **catch red handed**—catch someone in the middle of a criminal act

(2,15) **time is of the essence**—crucial, timing is very important, must do now

(3,19) **slip out**—go away without anyone noticing

(3,20) **stowaway**—to hide on a boat or train for a free ride

(3,20) **freeloaders**—people who ride without paying

(3,21) **take a chance**—accept the risk of loss or failure

(3,22) **be home free**—be certain to succeed because the worst is over

(4,24) **hit the road (hi-way)**—leave, often by car

(5,27) **wrapped up in**—to be thinking about or interested in only one thing

(5,28) **out of character**—unlike one's character

(5,29) **behind one's back**—sneakily; without one's consent

(5,29) **change one's mind**—change one's decision or opinion

(5,30) **mope around**—move around in a sad, depressed state
(5,30) **in touch**—write or talk to another, give or get news
(5,31) **get involved**—associated with someone, often romantically
(5,33) **snap(at)**—speak sharply to someone
(5,33) **don't you dare**—very angry if you do something I don't want you to do
(5,34) **head over heels**—completely or deeply in love with someone
(5,35) **lend a helping hand**—give someone help
(5,35) **water under the bridge**—something in the past that cannot be changed
(5,35) **get over it**—accept or forget something
(5,35) **tag along**—go with someone, often uninvited
(5,35) **fret**—worry or be concerned
(5,36) **tan one's hide**—give someone a beating
(6,40) **running away**—leave and not plan to come back, escape
(6,40) **leave alone**—stay away from, avoid
(6,40) **playing (around)**—fooling or joking
(6,40) **get along**—agree, cooperate, not fight or argue
(6,41) **hard feeling**—angry or bitter feeling
(6,41) **oldest trick in the book**—a way of deceiving someone that is not new
(7,46) **figured (out)**—find an answer by thinking about the question
(7,46) **big head**—too high of an opinion of your importance or ability
(7,46) **short (change)**—cheat, to return less to a customer than is due to them
(7,47) **over a barrel**—not able to do anything about what happens to you
(7,48) **get your butt up**—get over here right now
(7,49) **pass away**—die, have your life stop
(8,53) **worth his salt**—to be worth what one earns
(8,53) **full blast**—at full capacity
(9,58) **in the middle**—caught between two dangers
(9,58) **back burner**—a low priority
(9,58) **what is what**—what needs to be known, important facts
(9,58) **file charges**—make formal legal charges of wrongdoing against someone
(9,58) **round up**—collect or gather
(9,59) **come to the point**—get to or talk about the important facts of the matter
(9,59) **spy on**—watch someone to learn secret or concealed information
(9,61) **come forward**—to offer oneself or to tell
(9,61) **get together**—agree, gather together

(9,61) **hang around**—pass time or stay near with no special purpose
(9,62) **ring off the hook**—phone rings incessantly and repeatedly
(9,62) **drive one crazy (up the wall)**—to irritate or frustrate someone
(10,70) **head (for)**—go in the direction of
(10,71) **feel like**—want or have to do
(10,71) **live it up**—to pursue pleasure, have a good time
(10,71) **no comeback**—unable to answer or reply
(10,73) **hitch a ride**—get a free ride
(10,73) **make out**—see or understand
(10,75) **polish off**—finish quickly or completely
(10,76) **be history**—no longer present or relevant
(10,76) **sweet talk**—get what you want with flattery or praise
(10,76) **have a way with**—be able to lead or influence
(10,76) **spitting image**—exact likeness, duplicate
(10,78) **mind (watch) one's p's and q's**—be very careful what you do and say
(10,78) **hot water**—trouble
(11,81) **save one's hide**—save from danger or trouble
(11,82) **walk one through**—to lead someone through a process
(11,82) **out of sight**—not in one's field of vision
(11,83) **call around**—to telephone a number of people about something
(11,83) **hit the ground (running)**—be ready to start very energetically
(11,83) **mill around**—move impatiently in no particular direction
(11,85) **keep one's eye on**—watch carefully
(11,85) **hold it**—stop what one is doing
(11,85) **match for**—be equal to someone or something in a contest
(11,89) **hope for the best**—be optimistic about a situation
(11,85) **get a hold (grip) on**—take firm control of something
(11,94) **none of your business**—something that does not concern someone
(11,94) **bite off more than you can chew**—try to do more than you can
(11,94) **get going**—begin or start to move
(11,95) **by the way**—just some added news or fact
(12,98) **bring it up**—introduce a subject into discussion
(12,99) **under the circumstances**—in the present circumstances; as things are
(12,100) **bump into**—happen to meet; meet without expecting to
(12,100) **look after (someone)**—take care of; watch

Teacher Guide: Flight for Freedom / Karny Wilson Adventure Series Book One by M G Polk

(12,101) **bring up the rear**—to come last in the line or procession
(12,102) **as well as anyone**—in addition to; besides
(12,104) **eat and run**—eat a meal quickly and leave
(13,107) **shut out**—prevent from coming in
(13,107) **to one's self**— alone; away from others
(13,108) **get it**—understand
(13,108) **go over**—do again; repeat
(13,110) **look down his nose**—to think of as worthless; feel scorn for
(13,110) **rise and shine**—get up and get ready to go
(13,110) **head out**—leave; start out
(13,110) **lead the way**—guide; go first and show others how to go
(13,113) **good grief**—WOW; indication of surprise, good or bad
(13,113) **help oneself**—take what you want without asking
(13,114) **mess around**—play around or engage in idle activity
(13,114) **check out**—to make a list or record of things, observe
(13,114) **go through**—examine carefully; looking for something
(13,114) **try something**—test something
(13,115) **fit to a tee**—suit a person very well
(13,115) **give up**—surrender; quit trying
(13,115) **fast talker**—con artist; clever talker who convinces others easily
(13,115) **look for**—try to find; search for
(13,116) **first off**—right away; before anything else
(13,116) **last but not least**—in the last place but not the least important
(13,116) **keep an eye on (out)**—watch carefully; look for
(13,116) **here we are**—this is our situation right now
(13,116 **take one in**—take someone in to the police station for processing
(13,117) **get away**—get loose or get free
(13,117) **go easy on**—kind or gentle with someone or something
(14,119) **stay put**—stay in place; not move
(14,119) **work out**—get results; be efficient
(14,119) **dead giveaway**—something that reveals a fact or intention
(14,120) **risk one's neck (life)**—live dangerously
(14,120) **on his way**—on one's route to somewhere
(14,121) **beat up**—give a hard beating to; thrash
(14,122) **split second**—very short time; less than a second

(14,122) **dawn on**—become clear to
(14,122) **pay attention to**—hear and understand someone alertly; focus
(14,123) **set out**—to leave on a journey or voyage
(14,124) **head for**—go in the direction of
(14,127) **take on**—receive for carrying; be loaded with
(14,128) **in no time**—quickly; soon
(14,128) **kindred spirit**—resemblance to each other in many ways, including their ways of thinking and feeling
(14,130) **in hopes of**—expecting something
(14,130) **stick together**—stay close together in a situation
(14,133) **chip on one's shoulder**—easily angered; quarrelsome nature
(14,133) **raining cats and dogs**—rain very hard; come down in torrents
(14,134) **all the time**—very often; many times
(14,135) **mess with**—bother or interfere with someone or something
(14,136) **on one's mind**—in one's thoughts
(15,139) **off and on**—sometimes; not regularly
(15,140) **get ready**—prepare for something
(15,140) **sick and tired**—annoyed about something that has gone on too long
(15,141) **sure enough**—as expected
(15,144) **bring up**—take care of a child; raise; train
(15,144) **bit his tongue**—try hard not to say something one wants to say
(15,144) **pay one's way**—earn as much as you cost someone
(15,145) **in a bind**—in trouble
(15,145) **in harm's way**—in danger of being hurt or killed
(15,146) **in the long run**—in the end; final result
(16,148) **hold over**—postpone; delay action; keep things as they were
(16,148) **handouts**—free gift of food; clothing
(16,148) **make one's way**—do hard things to make a living; make life work
(16,149) **eyes open**—watch carefully; pay attention
(16,151) **left (you) alone**—stay away from
(16,152) **all out war**—total war
(16,152) **knock one's block (crown) off**—hit someone very hard
(16,153) **rub the wrong way**—bother; make a little angry
(16,153) **stopped dead in his tracks**—stop very quickly or with great force
(16,153) **out cold**—unconscious; in a faint

Teacher Guide: Flight for Freedom / Karny Wilson Adventure Series Book One by M G Polk

(16,157) **keep a civil tone**—speak decently and politely
(16,157) **to oneself**—silently; in one's thoughts
(16,158) **(run) work circles around**—do better than someone else
(16,159) **fudge (factor)**—margin of error; allow for changes
(16,160) **once over**—quick look; swift examination of someone or something
(16,161) **have a clue**—have a hint or know anything about a situation
(16,162) **in one's good graces**—approved of or liked
(16,162) **put up with**—accept patiently
(16,163) **square away**—arrange or properly take care of
(16,164) **bad apple**—one bad person in a group of people who are good
(16,164) **put in a good word for**—speak in favor of someone; recommend
(16,165) **better off**—richer; happier; in a better situation
(17,168) **shut your trap (face)**—stop talking
(17,170) **show the ropes**—explain to somebody how to do a job or activity
(17,170) **out of earshot**—too far away to be heard by the naked ear
(17,170) **take down a notch**—make someone less proud or sure of himself
(17,171) **mean nothing**—to have no effect or feeling for someone
(17,171) **cool it**—calm down; relax; take it easy
(17,171) **get busy**—accelerate the pace of one's activities
(18,176) **stick to**—follow; adhere to; obey
(18,180) **no (without a) doubt**—certainly; definitely; no questions
(18,182) **monkey business**—silly, comical tricks
(18,182) **pile in**—climb in or get in roughly
(18,182) **on the ball**—paying attention and doing things well
(18,183) **run-in**—violent quarrel
(18,185) **spread the word**—tell many people some kind of information
(18,185) **watch one's words**—be careful not to say anything rude
(19,188) **rat on**—betray; inform against; blow the whistle on
(19,188) **see the last of**—get rid of or say goodbye to someone or something
(19,190) **drop off**—take someone and leave them
(19,190) **in one piece**—not injured or damaged
(19,190) **shoot out**—fight with guns until one or side is wounded or killed
(19,190) **up against**—have trouble with someone or something
(20,193) **end up**—stop; come to an end; result
(20,193) **well put**—well expressed or defined

(20,194) **from time to time**—occasionally; not often
(20,195) **weigh on**—pressure or heavy on mind or thoughts
(20,195) **at hand**—within reach; nearby
(20,196) **have had enough**—have had as much as one needs of something; fed up
(20,196) **out of the way**—not where people usually go
(20,197) **get away with**—do something wrong without being punished
(20,197) **on top**—very close to; above
(20,197) **no chance**—no possibility something will happen
(20,198) **pin (down)**—trap someone or keep them from moving
(20,199) **under control**—manageable; not out of control
(21,202) **keep one's fingers crossed**—wish for good luck
(21,202) **fall in line**—stand properly in a row like soldiers; obey
(21,203) **catch up**—to find out about what you missed
(21,204) **like to have**—almost; just about
(21,205) **turn out**—prove to be; be in the end; grow into
(21,205) **go wrong**—fail; sink into criminal existence
(21,205) **get out**—leave or depart
(21,205) **out on bail**—released from prison because a security deposit known as "bail" has been put up by an individual or bail bond maker—bail is forfeited if the person flees.
(21,206) **break in**—robbery; burglary
(21,206) **run through**—read or practice from beginning to end
(21,206) **show up**—to come or bring out; make easy to see
(21,206) **fall off the wagon**—return to consumption of an addictive substance
(21,207) **keep up with**—be informed of the latest developments
(21,207) **break my heart**—cause someone great emotional pain
(21,207) **listen in**—eavesdrop
(21,207) **ill gotten gains**—goods or money obtained illegally
(21,208) **sort out**—clarify; figure out
(22,211) **stand for**—allow to happen or permit
(22,212) **on one's best behavior**—be as polite as possible
(22,215) **stick nose into**—prying or pestering interest in someone else's business
(22,216) **break one's heart (spirit)**—discourage greatly; make very sad
(22,217) **talk over one's head**—to say things one cannot understand
(22,218) **have in mind**—plan; intend; select; think about
(22,218) **take a look at**—examine someone or something

Colloquialisms

(1,3) **ain't**—am not; is not, are not; has not; have not

(1,6) **y'all**—you all

(2,10) **hit him**—understood or accepted an idea

(3,17) **you gonna be in a heap of trouble**—you will be in a great deal of trouble

(3,19 **ain't what's best**—is not good for someone

(4,25) **gave a good blessing out**—scold; rebuke

(5,27) **ain't seen hide nor hair**—have not seen someone for awhile

(5,28) **done been half blind fer years and near 'bout used up the other half**—only have 50% of my vision for a long time and am losing the remaining 50%

(5,36) **if'n you like I can stay over**—If you would like I can stay at your house

(6,40) **ain't for no trouble**—do not want to have any problems

(9,62) **lickity split**—moving very quickly

(10,70) **none of your beeswax**—none of your business

(10,77) **fixings**—accessories; necessary ingredients

(12,100) **ain't gonna get no time**—will not have any time

(12,101) **we are for no trouble**—we do not want any trouble or problems

(13,108) **rest your bones**—take time to rest or sleep

(13,110) **dimes worth of trouble**—very few problems

(13,111) **get along like peas and carrots**—always together, get along great

(14,125) **meaner than a snake**—very nasty or evil

(15,141) **why you hollerin'**—why are you yelling

(15,143) **leave you in a perilin' way**—desert you in a dangerous situation

(16,148) **gonna get kilt**—will be killed

(16,151) **upside of the head hello**—hit or strike on the side of the head

(16,154) **this ain't over**—this is not finished

(16,170) **whatta ya say**—what would you say about something

(16,173) **ain't no telling**—no way of knowing

(16,163) **knee high to a grasshopper**—to be very young

(17,167) **ain't gonna bite you**—not going to hurt you

(17,174) **I'll be doggone**—be surprised; shocked

(19,188) **ain't quite neighborly**—not friendly

(19,189) **have the sweets for**—feel fondness or affection for someone

(21,204) **like to have dropped**—almost dropped

Slang

(1,6) **blowhard**—empty boaster

(1,8) **whopper**—something big or remarkable; a big lie

(5,36) **high tail it**—go as fast as possible, especially in fleeing

(7,46) **moonshine**—very strong alcohol often made illegally

(10,68) **flatfoots**—police officers

(10,72) **ain't coming out of it anytime soon**—not changing the situation anytime soon

(10,74) **yap**—talk noisily or jabber

(10,76) **high tail it out**—leave in a hurry

(10,76) **pokey**—jail or prison

(10,77) **caloboose**—jail or prison

(11,88) **pull a job**—commit a crime, especially a robbery

(11,89) **got a whipping**—spanking

(13,116) **give someone some lip**—speak rudely or disrespectfully; sass

(14,124) **you ain't no cop are you**—are you a police officer?

(14,126) **grab some stuff**—steal from others

(14,139) **whatever**—informal way of showing indifference about a remark or idea

(14,141) **bunch of crock**—nonsense; foolishness

(15,146) **steer wrong**—mislead; give false information

(17,180) **up close and personal**—more intimately than one wants to be; in your face

(18,190) **on the street**—without a job; unemployed; without a place to live

(18,194) **kick some sense into**—beat someone to force them to do what you want

(18,197) **our cans**—buttocks

(18,198) **kick butt**—punish or defeat someone with a lot of force

(18,199) **let um have it**—attack someone physically or with words

(18,199) **give one a bad time**—criticize someone

(20,210) **sucker punch**—an unexpected blow; illegal blow

(20,213) **about you and me**—between you and me

(21,205) **below the radar**—undetected

(21,205) **con people**—deceive someone

(21,206) **do time**—serve a specific amount of time in prison

(21,206) **on the sly**—secretly and deceptively

(21,208) **pay back**—get even with someone for what they have done

Jargon

(2,10) **ox is in the ditch**—there is a big problem with unavoidable work ahead

(5,35) **come to Jesus meeting**—confront someone in trouble and insist they improve or be severely punished

(14,125) **present in spirit**—present in spirit although absent in body

(14,126) **Holy Roller**—one who attends a charismatic church service

(21,205) **devil got a hold of me**—I was overwhelmed by evil thoughts and gave in

(22,210) **once the circus gets in your blood, you are hooked for life**—once you begin to really enjoy the circus, you will always feel that way

Don't Miss The Next Exciting Karney Wilson Adventure!

Karney stopped and said, "I can't open it unless Naomi is here." He turned and walked to a side slit in the canvas of the big top. Naomi was standing in the center of the tent discussing her progress with the Flying Aces. Karny called out, "Excuse me, Naomi. I need to talk to you if you're not too busy. I got the letter from the Reds."

Naomi turned to the Aces and said, "Guys, this is really important. I'll be right back." She ran to Karny and joined the small crowd waiting for him to open his future.

Naomi was somewhat surprised to see the other four standing there looking like kids staring in the window of a candy store. Politely smiling, she said, "Hey, Mr. Wilson, Dad, Vernon, and you too Bobby. This is a very special occasion."

Karny slowly opened the envelope. He withdrew the letter and opened it to full length. He read it. Stopped and looked at all present. Then he read it again.

"Well, what does it say?" urged Vernon.

Without any expression, Karny handed the letter to Naomi. She read it to herself, and turned to look at her father. He saw her smile before. He saw her cry before. But, he never saw her overjoyed with tears. She screamed, "He made it! He made it!" Jumping up and down, she continued, "They want to sign him to a minor league contract. He made it. He made it."

She threw her arms around him and hugged him as tight as he had ever been hugged, except when he was wrestling someone. He had a smile across his face as he picked her up and spun her around as if she was as light as a rag doll.

Karny looked at his father who was wiping tears running down his face. He walked to him, put his arms around him, and said, "I love you, Dad."

Read more in "Making the Minors" Karny Wilson Adventure Series Book Two

www.ingramcontent.com/pod-product-compliance
Lightning Source LLC
Chambersburg PA
CBHW081800100526
44592CB00015B/2501